LIVING,
LEARNING,
HEALING

LIVING, LEARNING, HEALING

Inspirational Stories from the Heart

Diane L. Dunton, M.S., Reiki Master

Rainbow River Press

Rainbow River Press, Biddeford Pool, ME
© 2017 Diane L. Dunton
Dunton, Diane L., 1960 —
Living, Learning, Healing: Inspirational Stories from the Heart / Diane L. Dunton
Original trade paperback ISBN-13: 978-0-9823991-4-9
Library of Congress Control Number: 2016953407

Cover illustration and interior photos by Diane L. Dunton.
Book & cover design by Deb Tremper, SixPennyGraphics.com.

"Relay for Life: One Night's Journey" was originally published in *Sasee Magazine* (Strand Media Group), July 2009. "Build It Anyway" was first published in *Awareness Magazine*, Jan/Feb 2010.

For further information and permissions approval or to order copies of this book, go to www.dianedunton.com.

First Edition, 2017

Printed in the United States of America

DEDICATION

I dedicate this book to my supportive and loving daughters, Sara Deborah and Jessica Lynn. You are both so precious to me!

To Matt, Ian and Kaela, for who you are to me now and always.

To Jeff, my husband, for the routine, the unexpected, and the blanket of love you wrap me in each day. I am so enjoying this journey with you by my side.

For the four people I've known longest in this life, my siblings, Deb, Sally, Mike and Jodie. You are the embodiment of strength and courage. I am blessed to be your sister and aunt to your beautiful and loving children.

For my best friends, Donna, Janise, Marla, and my own Aunt Glo, your names invoke warmth and happiness and you've shown me both. Thanks for always being there to listen.

To Pat, my wonderful art teacher. You taught me that, "Paint is just paint," and we can change anything.

To Becky and Bob, whom we lost too soon.

And to my beloved grandson, Sawyer, you are my joy and hope for what is possible.

"I learned to watch the sunset and see the beauty unfold before my eyes. I cannot rush it or predict it. I need to be patient and allow myself to let go of expectations. Then, I wait for what comes and experience the joy and delight of the unexpected."

—Diane L. Dunton

Contents

FOREWORD

Every holiday season I look forward to my gift from Diane. In a simple large white envelope arrives a wall calendar for the coming new year, each month welcomed by a beautiful photograph skillfully taken and carefully selected by Diane.

Each photograph captures a compelling nuance of nature. From the delicate rainbow in a raindrop's prism to the reflection of a magnificent autumn sunset on a lake to the shimmer of sunlight on a dragonfly's wing, there is an invitation to view the world through Diane's insightful eye. Each photograph provides a glimpse into a curiosity, a reverence and a capacity to notice what the rest of us might otherwise overlook.

It is the lens of Diane's perspective that I have come to treasure and rely on over the nearly three decades of our friendship. Three decades that have witnessed the journey of *Living, Loving, Healing* she shares in this collection of stories. Diane applies this same photographer's focus to frame her life experiences, from the life-altering to the mundane, offering a perspective that provides clarity and meaning.

Diane will admit that she has faced far more than her fair share of personal tragedies—the untimely loss of cherished loved ones, painful estrangements and personal health issues. Time and again, I've witnessed her unique capacity to deeply experience and move through those events, arriving in a new place with positivity, optimism and deep conviction that the Universe will provide. I have marveled at her ability to reinvent herself continually with new mastery. Artist. Writer. Motivational Speaker. Reiki Master.

Friend. Mentor. Mirror. When faced with the inevitable personal or work challenge, I phone Diane knowing she'll offer an insight that will shift my perspective or pose a question that will illuminate a solution. While some of us may move through life collecting a sequence of experiences, Diane embraces those experiences—life's triumphs and tragedies—exploring their meaning, their impact and the possibilities they bring.

Coach. Counselor. Guide. Through this book, Diane shares her gifts of insight and understanding with all of us. Her wisdom, positivity and courage are etched into each story, providing us with hope and inspiration as we move through and make sense of our own unpredictable journeys.

—Marla Mosser, Organization Development Consultant
Center Valley, Pennsylvania
October, 2016

INTRODUCTION

We never know what life may send our way. Each journey is unique. When I was just six months old, my mother, Lila Adella, was told by doctors that I was not expected to live. At the time, she was a young woman living on a military base in Anchorage, Alaska. Alone and away from family, she had two other small children to tend. Though my mother had her share of challenges, she also possessed remarkable strength born of a deep faith that better days were just around the corner. She instilled this in me and it was perhaps her greatest gift.

In this, my first book, I write about survival, pain, joy, love, letting go, hope, fear, intention, giving back, positivity and dreams. At the most challenging times, I wished someone could throw me a life preserver. Only now, in retrospect, do I realize that someone did. My mother's gifts of strength and faith have buoyed me all along.

The following stories are ones of hope; hope that we can endure through impossible times.

It is possible.

—Diane L. Dunton, M.S., Reiki Master

ACKNOWLEDGEMENTS

When I first began to think about combining my passion for nature photography with my collection of inspirational essays, the necessity of having a team of people in place to support the project never occurred to me. Writing and photography seemed primarily solitary activities, but that was before I embarked in earnest on this project. I've learned a lot about publishing since this book's inception. Today, I know that successfully birthing a book requires the collaboration of a supportive team of people who are as equally passionate about the book as the author. I have been blessed with just such a team. Individually, each person has appeared in my life at the moment I needed him or her most. Collectively, they have provided invaluable guidance, encouragement, expertise and support along the journey. To each and every one, I am deeply grateful.

Always first, I thank my husband, Jeff Bruni. Jeff has given me unending and enthusiastic encouragement for this project. His willingness to read, critique and reread every draft was a labor of love. It is a wonderful thing to feel so fully supported by another human being. Jeff's steadfast companionship has made the work of this book joy-filled and my life's journey worthwhile.

My nephew, Ian Clough, has been so generous in dedicating time to the development of videography and other aspects of this project. His work has been invaluable and I am sincerely appreciative of both his time and talent.

Thank you to Barbara Delage, who gave me encouragement along the way and never wavered from believing in me and this book, and to Deb Tremper of Six Penny Graphics for her care and skill in creating the book's interior layout and cover design.

Many people graciously agreed to read the book's manuscript and provide feedback prior to publication, including Robert Fritz, Rev. David C. Hall, Dr. Hugh F. Harwood, Meredith Jordan, Katrina Kenison, Marla Mosser, Deborah Small and Martha Spruce. To them and others who will remain anonymous but gave me the courage to write and publish this book, many thanks.

Finally, I want to thank those willing souls who have found the courage in their own lives to face the unthinkable with a belief that trust in the Universe is all any of us really needs to make it through.

LIVING,
LEARNING,
HEALING

"Oh, the beauty. What a joy! The wind brushing lightly against my face..."

Great Falls Balloon Festival, August 2005.
Lewiston, Maine.

Living a Passionate Life: Take Flight

As a career coach, I have the opportunity to work with many people who have stayed in jobs despite suffering emotional, physical and psychological loss. When I receive a call from a potential new client, I hold on to their every word, knowing the courage it took for that person to reach out for help. Listening intently, I most often hear fear, hope and skepticism in their voices. "How can you help me," and "I don't know how to get started," are familiar words spoken time and again.

Why do people stay in jobs that are detrimental to their lives and wellbeing? Fear of the unknown and, more importantly, fear of loss, can keep people tied to jobs that leave them drained. Of course, these same fears can stand in the way of non-career changes as well. For instance, I have a fear of heights. I don't know when this fear arrived on my doorstep. It's just always been with me. I am a photographer and I love taking photos of hot air balloons. Taking photos from the ground is limiting. The lens of my camera can only achieve so much from standing under the balloons. I knew that, in order to capture a magnificent aerial shot, somewhere, sometime I would have to climb into a hot air balloon's basket and, untethered, become airborne—in spite of fear doing its best to keep me grounded.

In my professional life, I coach clients to take one step at a time as they learn to embrace change. In overcoming my own fear of heights, researching companies offering balloon rides was the first step. Eventually, I scheduled an appointment and traveled to a site in Vermont where balloons soar over beautiful gorges and majestic mountains. I learned that the best time of day for ballooning is first thing in the morning when the air is cool and the winds are gentle. My flight was scheduled for 6 a.m. on a beautiful June day. My stomach was filled with butterflies and my nerves were saying, *"Don't go!"*

As I climbed into the balloon, my hands were gripping the ropes while my feet were firmly planted in the basket. One, two, three and we were lifted off of the ground. The blast of hot air into the basket sent us higher and higher, yet ever so gently.

Oh, the beauty. What a joy! The wind brushing lightly against my face (a balloon speeds along at a mere two miles an hour). How could I ever have feared this? The sights below were magical; islands of trees in small ponds, mountain ranges, colors everywhere and the beautiful gorges.

One step of courage lifted me out of my fear. Fear can hold us back from trying new things, new jobs, new relationships or new experiences. Yet the fear is often much greater than the actual danger. Take one step to a new beginning and take flight!

Reflection Question: When has fear prevented you from trying something new? What might you do if fear did not hold you back?

"After I lost my husband, I wanted to paint, even though I had never painted before in my life."

Vulnerability, Authenticity and Passion

The ashes were still smoldering when the phone call woke me at 8 a.m. on a cold, brisk morning. I was shaking off sleep as I tried to absorb the words that were being shared on the other end of the line.

"The house burned to the ground," I managed to stammer out loud, adding, "Is everyone okay?"

The reply was a quiet, "I don't know if everyone got out."

Stunned, I quickly dressed and rushed to my car to drive the short one mile to where the fire occurred. There was the now homeless family, standing in the cold, wearing only pajamas and the jackets they'd grabbed on their way out of the blazing structure. They stood together, looking at what was left of their home and business. With one family member recovering from cancer, the devastation of another tragedy for this family was hard to comprehend. Yet everyone was safe, including the family's cats.

In the following days, the community surrounded the family with an outpouring of love, food, clothing and offers of shelter. The family had a hard time accepting all of the well wishes, gifts and visits, including those from complete strangers who offered a hand.

Why do so many of us have a hard time accepting support? Why do we find it so difficult to be in a position to need the help of others? My belief is that when we need help due to a devastating fire, a job loss, a divorce, a death in our family or a diagnosis of a serious illness, we become vulnerable. When we are vulnerable we are left with just our core being exposed. For many of us, this is when we are our most authentic self. We cannot hide, we cannot mask what is happening to us and, even though we may push it away, we need the help of others.

I have written many articles over the years encouraging readers to create a vision for themselves and look at what they are passionate about in their life and work. I do the same with clients. Often, if we reflect on those times in our lives when we have been at our most vulnerable and authentic, we will see where our passion lies. When we are vulnerable, we are often forced to look at what and who matters most to us, and reflect on how we want to spend our time.

After I lost my husband to cancer, I wanted to paint, even though I had never painted before in my life. I reached out to a local artist who, thankfully, helped me get started. That was many years ago and today I'm still painting. After my own journey with breast cancer, I wanted to write and share my experiences and stories with others, and so I began a blog. When we are vulnerable, we may open up to new opportunities that allow our passion and our true authentic self to shine through for all to see. Most importantly, it allows us to understand and see our core self.

I hope you are finding your passion through allowing yourself to be vulnerable and authentic and searching your soul for what motivates you in your work, relationships and life.

Reflection Question: When have you felt vulnerable? When did you need help? Did your vulnerability show what you are passionate about? If so, how can you bring that passion into your life?

"I planted a rose in remembrance of
our love and the life we shared."

Diane's Garden, 2010.
Windham, Maine.

Joy/Pain...Living in Both

November 15th is my late husband's birthday. It's a day to celebrate, but it's also a day of sadness. My husband passed away from a fast-growing cancer in 2002. This is a day of joy and pain. Joy and celebration of the short time we had together and pain of the loss of the life we shared.

After Bob's death, I found life pulled me along, sometimes with me taking only one baby step at a time. There were moments when I didn't know if I could get up to face another day, but each evening I would watch the setting sun—one of the Universe's beautiful gifts—and reflect upon the joy and pain of the day.

At times in my life, I've experienced a dichotomy of joy and pain. I started one week listening to a man speak gently about his 90-year-old father. The father, he described to me, was in a state of joy, of delight. He had just found out that he had a serious health issue and the only resolution was surgery or death. If he did not have the surgery, he would die in a week or a few months. He was delighted! His fear was that he would have a slow, lingering death. Now, he knew it would be quick. This was one man's joy.

On the same day, I saw a beautiful young woman who had been beaten badly in a relationship that had gone out of control. Her face was bruised, her heart broken and her pain deep. Tears came to my eyes as I listened, watched and held her heart in my heart. With the pain, she was also experiencing joy; the joy of a new life and new possibilities and the joy of friends and family who were surrounding her with love.

Through the years, I have listened to the deep pain of friends and colleagues. I have also heard words of joy and hope for the days to come. With the pain comes the promise and hope for a new day.

Be sure to cry the tears of pain and the tears of joy. Each day, the beauty of the rising sun will remind you of the beauty of the day gone by. Embrace the moment. Find and hold those moments that give you joy.

Reflection Questions: Where are you experiencing pain in your life? Where do you see joy as a sign of hope for your future? Is it in the rising sun, in a flower holding on before the arrival of cold winter days, in the beauty of a sunset or in the sound of laughter from a child?

"Remember to hold on, knowing
the storms will pass.

Build It Anyway

As I sat in the audience of Martina McBride's holiday concert, I had no idea how moved I was about to become. Dressed in a dazzling white gown which reflected the bright stage lights, the country superstar was radiant. She opened the show with a new song, one that would soon appear on her latest album and attach itself to me in a way that no song had done in years. It was a song about possibilities and dreams—a song commanding the listener to never give up. Even now, years later, the echo of "Anyway" reverberates, urging me to follow my passion no matter what life throws my way. Dream it anyway. Build it anyway. Just keep going.

As a career coach, my wish is that my clients keep Martina's lyrics as a mantra; that no matter what obstacles they face, they might hold tight to their dreams and find the strength to *do it anyway*. As a professional consultant, I have been privileged to bear witness to the dreams and desires of countless people over the years. My clients have shared their dreams and hopes and passions, and I have yet to encounter any one dream that lacks possibility. These are dreams that are possible to achieve in this lifetime. So many of us dream and then let our dreams go because of fear; fear of taking that first step, fear of the unknown, fear of trusting.

The lyric "build it anyway" elicits a strong emotion in me. I married in my early twenties with the dream of possibilities. We had two children before my first storm came. The union struggled and I found myself divorced and alone with two small children depending on me. There were dark days when I did not think that I could get up, but I did and I built my family in a new and different way.

My next tempest came when my mother, my mentor, who had instilled in me the confidence to go after every dream, was diagnosed with a malignant brain tumor. As I faced what lay ahead, I struggled with many questions. I had just started a master's degree program, was still a single mom and was working a full-time job that required a lot of travel. Though many demands were already on me, I knew that my mother would need me to help care for her in the ensuing months.

One day, as we sat on my back porch with the crisp fall air embracing us and knowing that I had precious little time with her, I asked her, "*What do I do?*" She replied, so matter of fact and knowing, "*You continue taking classes and get your degree.*"

She left this earthly world within ten months of that conversation and, six years later, I received my degree. I did it anyway. And she was smiling down on me. At the time, I thought losing my mom was the biggest storm I would have to face in my lifetime. Fate had other plans.

While pursuing my degree, I had another dream to start my own consulting business. In 1996, six months after my mother had passed away, I opened the doors to Potential Released Consulting

Services. My desire was to help individuals, groups and organizations release their potential and, like a magnificent hot air balloon, take flight!

Fast forward five years later and my business and my life were going well. I was remarried to a wonderful man, my daughters were growing into lovely young women and life was good. I had gotten through the anxious moments at the start of my business when I would ask myself questions like, *Can I really do this*, and *Will people find my services valuable?* But the business took off and I was passionate about the work.

Just when I thought my dream life had been built, another storm came along. My beloved husband was diagnosed with cancer. During his illness, I let the dream of my business go. I spent my time (with no regrets) caring for and being with him. He passed within the year.

After he passed, I still had my dream. I had no business left, but the dream remained, and so I rebuilt. New storms were swirling all around me—one of my sisters died of cancer, another sister was battling the disease, and a brother was diagnosed with a benign brain tumor; yet I stood strong in the eye of the storm. I dreamt and built it anyway.

With each passing storm comes a gift. In the midst of a storm, I don't always know what that gift is, but it does come. After my mother passed, I left a company I had been with for 20 years and started my own business. After my husband died, I pursued my dream of having an art studio and began painting and rebuilding my business. My consulting practice is going strong now. The storms have come and gone.

While pursuing my dreams, I have witnessed and assisted others in building theirs. I feel privileged to listen to others and be able to create an environment for them to make their dreams a reality.

One woman I worked with started a business offering planned vacations for busy professional women, connecting them with each other and the arts all across the country. A man started a soap and candle business after leaving a distribution position he had held for years. Another woman left a corporate position to become a teacher and work with kindergarten children. All had dreams and storms along the way.

We must remember to hold on, knowing the storms will pass.

I continue to support people who are dreaming and I know that if they dream, they can build. They can make it through the storms.

> **Reflection Question:** What is your dream? What do you want to build? What might be stopping you from realizing your dream? Storms will come and they will pass. Begin to build today.

*"Walk your path
and carry the hope."*

Hope at Relay for Life, 2010.
Windham, Maine.

Relay for Life: One Night's Journey

Every spring, the American Cancer Society's Relay for Life® event is held in remembrance of the cancer victims we've lost and as hope for a cure for those living with the disease. I hate cancer. Cancer has taken so many close to me....friends, mother, in-laws, sister and husband. Every year, I commit to the Relay in ink on my calendar and begin gathering teammates and other participants for the event.

The 16-hour trek starts on a Friday at 6:00 p.m. and ends with a closing ceremony sometime between 10:00 a.m. and noon the next day. These events are held all over the country and involve survivors, caretakers, teams, friends and family members. In my case, the walk is held in the beautiful state of Maine.

I am always too slow in getting pledges, as if to say on some subconscious level, *"We don't need this event."* As I begin to design the white bags that will later be filled with sand to hold them down and a candle which will burn through the night, I reflect on the Relay's importance. I decorate a bag for each person who has been affected by cancer and has touched my life. I personalize each bag with pictures, drawings, sayings or just words that create a visual for each person.

I pack my tent and layers of clothing (here in Maine the wee hours of the morning can be very cold, sometimes 30 degrees Fahrenheit). We may endure rain, fog, thundershowers and, in some years, hail. Clothing, therefore, needs to address all possible conditions.

As I arrive at the high school track that has so graciously offered their space, this year appears no different than others. Teams are putting up their tents. Vendors are offering coffee, burgers and other treats. Luminary bags are being set up by volunteers along the inside edge of the track. The night's preparations are being made.

At the opening ceremony I listen as my sister, chairperson for this year's walk, shares the importance of the Relay and what we are all about to undertake over the next 16 hours. A moving story by a couple, both cancer survivors, creates a sense of hope. Then, the talking stops and the first walk around the track begins. Survivors, with medallions around their necks marking the number of years they have participated, and their caretakers are the first and only ones to walk that opening lap. The young, the old and those with radiation or chemotherapy-induced bald heads all walk together. Teams, family members and friends cheer and clap vigorously from the sidelines.

My first Relay was three months after my late husband was diagnosed with pancreatic cancer. He passed in 2002, but even now I look forward to the annual walk, though I'm never quite sure what the night's emotional impact will be on me. Each year, the faces, once again, remind me that cancer affects so many. They tell a story of triumph, true human will and courage.

During the first year, my team included my two daughters, my sister, a niece, my stepfather and several friends. The plan was that we would walk all night. We would pitch our tent, decorate our site with the theme of the power of purple, set our lawn chairs by the track and begin walking.

The team next to our campsite was selling, as part of a donation, nylon string to hold beads. Each trip around the track upon passing their site, we would take a bead to mark that lap. This would prove to be a great motivator as our legs began to tire during the long night!

Even though only one team member is required to be on the track at all times, my team members and I made a pact to walk together throughout the event.

The time is 6:45 p.m. and we begin walking. I am energized, despite the fact that seasonal allergies have plagued me all day and I can't stop sneezing. I know I am doing my part to raise awareness in the fight against cancer. The night may be long, but well worth our efforts.

At 9:00 p.m., volunteers begin lighting the candles inside each bag. The track is completely lined with bags that will burn brightly throughout the night. They keep me motivated...one each for my mom, my husband, the grandparents of my children, my sister, two good friends and a woman from a local bank who is special to me. Their names and pictures are on the bags with the words *in memory of* or *in honor of.* These keep me going long into the night.

At 9:30 p.m., each team reads aloud the names of the people on their bags. The sound echoes in the stillness of the night. This year, it takes almost an hour to read all of the names, many of whom are strangers to me. As the names are read, the walk continues in silence. Some walkers pause by a luminary of a dear one. Tears are shed, soft-spoken words are uttered, or a prayer or laughter is offered up as remembrances are shared. Off to the side on a hill, luminaries spell out the word HOPE. At the end of the reading, the bags on the hill are quickly rearranged to spell the word CURE.

After this part of the event is done, the DJ takes over with lively music, talking heightens again and walkers resume their pace. The smell of doughnuts and coffee fill the air and pizza, always a favorite, is brought in at midnight. I walk with one daughter, sometimes both, sometimes with my stepdad and sometimes alone.

As the night progresses, blisters begin to form on my feet. I have been walking previous to this night, but not this distance. My sneakers start to lose their comfortable feel. At 1:00 a.m., I have collected 40 beads, equaling 10 miles! There are several hours left and I am curious how many beads I will have by the end of the event.

At 2 a.m., I begin to slow down. The tendons behind my left knee hurt. I change my shoes to see if it helps. It doesn't. I go back to my worn sneakers. My oldest daughter, who is plagued by a bad back, decides to take a break and lie down for a while. Many have long since retired to their tents or cars for a few hours of sleep. My youngest daughter, stepdad and I keep walking.

At 2:30 a.m., not only have I hit a wall, I feel like I've smacked right into it. My legs and hips hurt. My sneakers provide little support to my tired feet. *Can I keep going? Will I see the morning sunrise? Will I succumb to the sleeping bag that awaits me in our tent?*

At 3 a.m., my daughter and I decide to run. YES, RUN! We think it may loosen our muscles and tight tendons. We run for 45 minutes. We pick up speed. I feel like I am sailing around the track. I am renewed! I have broken through the wall and have new energy, weaving around the walkers spaced intermittently on the track.

At 4:30 a.m., the first signs of early morning daylight begin to emerge. Soon I hear the sweet sounds of birds stirring. At the first chirps, I know I have almost made it. I remind myself of all the pain, aches and suffering people who have cancer endure. This is one night that I can endure in their memory and honor.

The sun begins to rise. Sleepy faces emerge from tents and take to the track again. I feel exhilarated! I count 72 beads. That's 18 miles! My daughter thinks we should try for 104 beads or 26 miles. I look at her like she has two heads, but I agree to try. She has helped keep me motivated throughout the night, so I will keep going. The blisters on my feet hurt. My hips provide little support to my tired body. My sneakers feel like weights. I keep going.

In the end, I collect 94 beads, white, purple and clear, one for each lap I walked; a total of 23.5 miles. My daughter and stepdad collected 104...26 miles. I limp around my last lap hoping that I won't disappoint those I held in my heart all night long. I did this for each one of them.

The Relay comes to an end. As I load my things into the car, I realize that I have not failed. I have succeeded in raising money and awareness for cancer and helping, in my own way, change HOPE to CURE.

For those I've lost, Mom, Becky, Bob, Nanny and Bampi, this night was for you; and for Maureen, Diana, Lex and Deb, as you continue to walk your path and carry the hope; and for the many others, known to me only through the luminaries that burned so brightly through the night.

Reflection Question: Life presents challenges to us. When have you had to push through? When have you endured emotional or physical pain and overcome it?

"I know I have my part to play and yet, in trusting the Universe, all things are possible."

Cody, 2006.
Mixed media, oil on acrylic.

Intentions Versus Resolutions

I'm sure you've read articles on New Year's resolutions and how to be successful in the New Year. My thought is this: if resolutions have not worked in the past, then they probably are not going to work any better this year. Why do we make resolutions? What does "resolution" mean? What would happen if we were to reframe our thinking to make *intentions* instead?

According to Merriam-Webster, a resolution is an act or process of answering or determining. In essence, it is to solve something. We make resolutions to lose weight, get a new job, be more attentive to our relationships or be more organized, to name a few. The assumption is that something—usually involving our own behavior—is not working for us and needs to be stopped or started. Often, resolutions do not work because they reside in a frame of mind that tells us there is a problem to be solved. We come to terms with the problem, reconcile ourselves to solve the problem and then create an action plan. If there is no consequence to the problem, most of us will not create an action plan to solve it. The stated resolution, although a nice thought, goes by the wayside.

What if we reframed our thinking and stated what we wanted to accomplish in terms of intentions for the year? An intention is something one hopes to accomplish or bring about. The focus is on the future rather than the past. The focus is on possibilities, not solving old problems. The focus is on hope, not on what hasn't worked.

I believe in intentions. I believe that if we state our intentions and put them into the Universe, the Universe responds. An intention is positive and hopeful. It's about possibilities. The Universe will respond if we clearly state what we hope to bring about in the year. This is not just semantics; it is a state of mind.

In 2003, my intention was to begin painting. I signed up for an art class with a local artist. I had never painted before. I started with acrylics and then moved on to oils. I had lost my husband the previous fall and my grief was overwhelming. Our life together was planned and, suddenly, he was diagnosed with pancreatic cancer. Eight months later, he left this world. I needed to rebuild my world and I started with painting.

I had told my husband that I wanted to be able to paint the photos that I loved to take. When I walked into that art class, my shaky nerves and lack of self-confidence were palpable. But, I kept at it.

In 2006, one of my intentions was to be acknowledged by others for my artwork and have commissioned work. That year I had four commissioned pieces! I gave my intention to the Universe and the Universe responded. I have deep gratitude and take the time each day to thank the Universe for what I have received. (You can view some of my work online at dianedunton.com.)

Looking ahead, my intentions are to bring about new possibilities for myself. I trust in the Universe. I trust in the positive energy that will come my way. I know I have my part to play and yet, in trusting the Universe, all things are possible.

Instead of setting resolutions each year, write your intentions, give them to the Universe and enjoy a prosperous and Happy New Year!

Reflection Question: How do you start each year? Do you lament over old problems or look to the future? What are your intentions?

"This will not be without struggles, pain or sadness, but I have no choice. My journey has begun."

Rattlesnake Mountain, October 2015,
Raymond, Maine.

An Unexpected Journey Begins

Beep....beep....beep....da...da....da...
"Just three more minutes." The voice
came faintly through the headset.
DA...DA...DA...DAAAAA...
"One more time."
They were right; it did sound like a jackhammer.
Silence. Then, a voice.
"Now you will feel the dye in your arm. It may be cold."

I love the fall season; bright, cerulean blue skies, crisp, clear air and colors that create a reminder of nature's brilliance. I look forward to it. I spend hours planting colorful mums to faded gardens, tucking summer toys and lawn furniture away in the shed and preparing for that inevitable first snowfall.

Living at the edge of a beautiful Maine lake, quietness settles over our community each fall. Busy visitor traffic to the lakeside cottages slows and there are fewer people out for walks along the dirt road. The boats are pulled from their summer moorings and docks are taken out of the water and stacked for the long winter.

The water is much lower and the loons begin dancing spiritedly in the bay as if to proclaim, *The lake is ours again.* A long beach emerges, urging the year-round residents to take full advantage of walking the water's edge and watching the loons at play.

Beep...beep...beep...DA...Da...Da...

"Okay, Diane, two more sets."

I listen to Faith Hill, barely audible through the

headset, singing, "Breathe...just breathe."

"How did things change so quickly?" I silently wonder.

2007 is a transformative year. Physically, I am in the best shape since my husband passed away five years ago. After losing the thirty pounds of excess weight that was causing my lungs to work extra hard, I am running four times a week, three to four miles at a time and eating wholesome food. I feel energized, never believing that I could lose the weight, run again or regain the strength I had in years past. I feel healthy and invigorated. I am strong.

"Diane, this isn't the news you wanted

to hear. You have cancer."

The words left my doctor's mouth, shot through the phone line and exploded my tranquil life like a bombshell.

"What? You must be talking about someone else," I wanted to scream, but the words stayed in my head without leaving my lips. Instead, my voice spoke calmly. *"Okay. What's next?"* Tears silently escaped my eyes.

Since that day, I have stepped onto "the conveyor belt of the medical world," as one dear friend put it. Despite caring for so many of my own family members with cancer, the word itself still shocked, because now they were talking about me. After all of my biopsies, I still wasn't ready for this. *I'm the caretaker. How will I do this? How will I let others care for me?*

After the news, I meet with oncologists and surgeons. I've had MRI's and time to think—and too much of it alone. Time is not going fast enough. I have decided to have a bilateral mastectomy. I am losing a part of me—a loss that I've grieved since I made the decision—yet I know it's the right one for me.

I am busy cancelling business appointments and replacing them with medical visits, massages and whatever else I may need. As I plan for a future that was not part of my plan, I think, *I am healthy! I am a runner! I lost weight! How could this have happened?*

Even though my core is still healthy, the cancer is in me. I cannot see it or feel it, but they tell me it is there. As the beautiful fall weather sets in, my life begins an unexpected course. It feels surreal. I am supposed to be doing other things, not postponing work and activities until some unknown future date.

Instead, I am trusting in the Universe that I am right where I am supposed to be at this time in my life, complete with tears and laughter. This will not be without struggles, pain or sadness, but I have no choice. My journey has begun.

Reflection Question: When have you had unexpected news? In what way did you put trust in the Universe?

"When the time is right, I hear her
signal and the male arrives."

Diane's Yard, 2016.
Windham, Maine.

Taking Risk...Taking Flight

Have you ever watched the flurry of activity at birdfeeders as birds come and go? Throughout my life, wherever I have lived, I've found great joy in setting bird feeders in place and watching the routine of new birds discovering them.

Each type of bird has their particular dance to the feeder. The white and black chickadees dart in and out quickly, snatching a seed or two and retreating to the bushes. The tufted titmouse, similar to the chickadee, flies, takes seeds and departs. Both of these birds take several trips until their mission is accomplished.

The bright yellow and black male goldfinches fly in with grace; they ease and linger for a time, while dancing between the feeders. As many as 30 goldfinches may perch themselves on the feeders and take their time gathering the finch food or sunflower chips. They continue to do this until they are full of the sustenance.

The blue jay is bold and it dominates whenever approaching the feeders. Other birds give the blue jay the respect warranted for such a large, bold feeder. The call of the blue jay announces his arrival. He takes what he wants and leaves quickly.

The cardinals intrigue me the most. The sheer beauty of the red male with its black coloring around the face captures my attention. I will sit for long periods of time (and I am not a patient person for sitting) with my camera in hand waiting for a shot of the cardinal.

The female and male cardinals' dance to the feeder is fascinating. At the same time each day, I hear the female emitting her sounds, announcing that it is time to travel to the feeder. As she approaches, her sounds become louder, announcing her arrival. She is beautiful in her own right, a mélange of taupe and orange colors subtly displayed as she sits in the nearby bushes checking the feeder for safety.

The female determines when the male cardinal should proceed to the feeder. He will not arrive before she signals with sounds that all is well. This takes some time, which is why, if I want to photograph the male, I must sit still and wait. Their dance is one of total trust and partnership with each other. When the time is right, I hear her signal and the male arrives on the ground. Very rarely does he land on the feeder itself. He feeds from the leftovers dropped by the other visitors.

The cardinals, unlike the bold blue jays or goldfinches, are not risk takers. They wait, circling, flying in and perching on nearby bushes, watching for the right, often brief, moment to take their treasure. Sometimes, they never even get to the feeder because something causes them to retreat.

As a career coach, I have encountered many people who, like the cardinals, want to take risk and find what might await them, but are not quite daring enough. Some days, the cardinals lose their opportunity because they waited too long. They are unable to gather the food that they need for their own survival.

Recently, I sat with a woman whose life over the past few years has not been easy. She had cared lovingly and gently for her husband whose health was failing, until he passed away. I listened as she told me of a passion that she wanted to bring to fruition. Her face was light and she spoke with such determination and excitement. This opportunity would require her to take risk. Without taking risk, she could not achieve the passion that was swelling in her very being.

I received an email from her two days later. She shared with me all of the many steps she had taken in just two days. She is well on her way to achieving her goals.

How many of us look at the beauty of a passion and have desire for it, but are not willing to step out of our comfortable world and take the risk to achieve our heart and soul's desire? The cardinal is a bird of beauty that often leaves without fulfilling its daily need for fuel.

Reflection Questions: What risk are you willing to take in your life to fuel your own sustenance for your soul? What step can you take, even if it is a small step? Who can support you?

"Time has been my friend."

Bailey at Pine Point, 2007.
Old Orchard Beach, Maine.

All about Time

*"Life is so busy. I can't seem to get it all
done. I need more hours in a day."*

How often do we hear these words? We live in a world where it has almost become a status symbol to say, "I am so busy." I am guilty of this myself. I never seem to have enough time to write, market my business, paint or work on all of the endless projects I have around my house. I never have enough time.

And yet, since the diagnosis of my cancer, the hours pass slowly. Time cannot move fast enough. I am waiting for my surgery; a surgery that will change my body image, my sense of who I am physically and, at the same time, potentially save my life. I am lucky. The cancer in my breast has been caught early. I have been diligent about regular checkups and multiple biopsies, always remembering my sister, whom we lost to breast cancer.

But I didn't expect the days to go by so slowly. Like most, I tidy up before I take a trip or a vacation. This waiting for surgery has the same feel. I have cleaned my office, washed windows at home and organized my art supplies. These are all tasks that are long overdue and I feel an urgent need to complete then now.

I denied that I would ever face this journey. I used to think, *"Two sisters with cancer, but it will skip me. I am healthy. I am strong."* Well, I was wrong. This journey has begun.

No matter how busy I try to be, the days still have 24 hours to them. I have lots of time right now to think, to reflect and to just be. As the sun sets, I wait and wonder, *"What will my life be like on the other side of surgery?"*

All we have is this moment. How can I best use this time? Today is the day before my surgery, and I feel peaceful. The waiting has almost passed. I walked on the beach today with a loved one and my two favorite puppies. I photographed a horse running through the ocean waves. I watched a rainbow with all of its magic appear in the sky.

Just a few more hours left to this beautiful, wonderful, peaceful day. As I look forward to a new beginning, I know that time has been my friend. And soon I'll have time to not only watch rainbows, but to look for the gold.

Reflection Questions: When have you felt time moved too quickly or slowly? When have you felt too busy? What is your relationship with time?

"I felt a peace wash over me."

Jordan Bay in February, 2016.
Sebago Lake, Windham, Maine.

Being Still and Letting Go

As I catch my reflection in the mirror, outwardly I appear the same as I did before my cancer surgery. Hair flowing softly around my face, a body that reflects a year of devotion to exercise and a smile that appears when people ask me how I am doing. Inwardly, I am changing and healing in ways that I do not even fully know. I reflect and spend many moments being still. Being still allows my body to work hard and heal, but it is a difficult challenge for me. My body needs rest, yet my mind, even in the wee hours of morning light, is unable.

What about my work? What about my clients? How will I decorate my home for the holidays? How will I prepare for the holidays? How will I pay bills and keep up with things during this time of no work as a business owner who is self-employed? When will I be able to pick up a paint brush and add strokes to a canvas?

My arms tire easily just from writing or responding to emails, yet my mind is racing. Three weeks have passed since my surgery; a surgery that freed my body of breast cancer; a surgery that freed me from the threat, anxiety and gray cloud that loomed over my head during 20 years of biopsies.

On the day of my surgery, I felt a peace wash over me. No more breast biopsies. The bilateral mastectomy would take that risk away along with the cancer.

New challenges began in the first two weeks after the surgery. Tiny movements of my arms and chest muscles proved difficult. I have been amazed at how much we use our chest muscles to do the simplest of tasks; I always thought my arms alone were doing the heavy lifting. Now, turning on the kitchen faucet with the necessary push/pull movement seems nearly impossible. Daily tasks, such as opening doors, reaching for a coffee mug on a shelf above shoulder height, or trying to wash and dry my hair not only take longer, but in attempting them my body feels as if it is moving in slow motion. Allowing my family to help me with even the simplest of tasks, like bathing, has challenged me to let go.

Humor has gotten me through some of the toughest moments. Family members have competed over who can style my hair the best (my oldest daughter won that contest), who is the better driver (my youngest daughter) and how to wash my hair without getting the bandages wet (I will keep the winner of that task a secret!).

As I begin to heal inside, I need to give myself credit for what I can do at this early stage. I need to give myself permission to take it easy. Naps (several in a day, if necessary) are a good thing. I'm healing. In my normal, fast-paced world, being still and patient doesn't come easy. It's time to let go of the unreasonably high expectations I have of myself.

And then, there is the external. The reconstructive process for my body has barely begun. As I look at it, the changed image is hard to view. Stitches, swelling and bruising are prominent. I am disfigured in a way that my eyes are not ready to see. As an artist, there is a certain point in a painting when I want to toss whatever I am working on into the trash. Thankfully, I hesitate to do this. Most often, if I continue to work, the painting transforms into a finished and beautiful piece of art.

My wise daughter of 23 years reminded me of what transpires when I paint. She said, *"Mom, your body, like your paintings, is just beginning to transform. You will be beautiful."*

Yes, if I can let go, be patient, remain still and allow the healing, reflecting and learning to happen, it will be good. Laughing at the little things that I find challenging will help to get me through it. As I write this on Thanksgiving Day, I know I have much to give thanks for this year.

Reflection Question: At certain times in our lives, we need to be still. When have you needed to be still? Did you find practicing stillness difficult? What did you learn about yourself?

"I sit down to snuggle with my grandson,
and we delight in the little bear together."

Pooh Bear at Home, 2011.
Windham, Maine.

Growing Takes Courage

*"Promise me you'll always remember: You're braver than you
believe, and stronger than you seem, and smarter than you think."*
- A.A. Milne

As a young girl, I fell in love with Winnie the Pooh and his friends, Piglet, Eeyore and Tigger. My childhood nickname, Poodie, drew me even closer to him. Pooh was carefree. He paused to reflect on the simplest things in life and he had one primary focus: honey. Oh, honey brought such joy to that little round, cuddly, yellow bear. But as I matured, it seemed to me that our names were all we had in common. I would later discover how much I needed Pooh.

Throughout my teens and early twenties, I lost touch with Pooh and my reflective, curious side. Intense, driven and out to make my mark on the world, I was elected the first freshman chair of Student Activities while in college. I worked hard in my classes and created a strong network of friends. Upon graduation, I jumped right into a management training program with a Fortune

500 company and began pursuing what was my goal of climbing the corporate ladder.

When my two precious daughters came into the world in my late twenties, I introduced them to Pooh's adventures through bedtime stories. I reconnected and fell in love with Pooh all over again. We read the questions that Winnie the Pooh posed to his friend Christopher Robin, considered Pooh's responses to his less than optimistic friend, Eeyore, and enjoyed the sheer delight Pooh found in sharing with friends. Seeing the joy in my daughters' bright eyes as we laughed at silly Pooh reminded me to hold on to the delight of the simple and see what curiosity can bring. I even painted a life-sized Pooh and Piglet on my children's playroom wall.

Eventually, our reading time with Pooh slipped away as my daughters outgrew their playroom. When we moved, we said goodbye to our life-sized friends from the Hundred Acre Wood, who were probably painted over by the new owners. Time escaped me. Life moved on and I was busy.

On a trip to Disney with my daughters ten years later, a stuffed Pooh in a souvenir store caught my attention. As I walked by the display of Pooh sitting graciously on a chair with an indiscriminate look about him, I reminisced to my daughters about my favorite character. My oldest daughter, watching me, finally blurted out, *"Mom, why don't you treat yourself and buy Pooh? You know how you love him."*

"How silly of her," I thought. *"I'm a grown woman! I couldn't buy Pooh for myself. I wouldn't have the room in my suitcase to carry him back home. I shouldn't spend the extra money; that's for souvenirs for the girls or family back home."*

Then, in an instant, I knew I couldn't leave him behind. I picked up the soft bear and headed to the register. Pooh was still my love and now, once again, my home would be his.

As my life became busy again, Pooh remained a fixture on a chair in my bedroom. Pooh changed chairs when I subsequently moved to new homes, but he always made his presence felt. He was a reminder that, even in an unfamiliar place, I will recognize what is truly important.

As I began thinking about writing this chapter, the word "courage" came to mind. Throughout my recovery from breast cancer, the word "courage" has been said to me over and over by friends, particularly around my decision to have a bilateral mastectomy.

Webster's defines courage as "mental or moral strength to venture, persevere and withstand danger, fear, or difficulty." As I searched the internet for quotes on courage, my old friend Pooh appeared as one of the first quotes on the list: "Promise me you'll always remember: You're braver than you believe, and stronger than you seem, and smarter than you think."

Comparing myself to heroes or heroines throughout history, I noticed that I just did what I knew I needed to do. I was braver than I believed possible for me, stronger than I seemed to ever have been before. Suddenly Pooh's quote put it in simple terms for me. I *have* been courageous and I *have* been brave.

That is the human spirit. We all have that strength in us: to apply the courage and bravery from within. It's resting, just waiting for the moment in which it is needed and then it shines. I have seen the spirit shine in others in their darkest moments. It's a part of each of us.

Yes, Pooh, I do have courage. I have been brave. Thank you, Pooh, and to my friends for stating it so simply. I have been more courageous than I believed I could ever be as I have traveled on my cancer journey. I know I will continue to be brave as I continue to heal.

"*This one?*" I ask.

"*Yes, Mema!*" says Sawyer.

I pull the Pooh story from the shelf and sit down to snuggle with my grandson, and we delight in the little bear together.

Reflection Questions: When have you had to show courage? What did you lean into? Who helped you?

"Can you be a hero for one person today?"

Loons, August 2013.
Long Lake, Naples, Maine.

How Two Modern Day Heroines Made a Difference

The young woman waited patiently until the store closed before moving quietly toward the dumpster. She knew well that the store personnel threw out the leftover food that she would salvage and give away to people in need. The need on some days overwhelmed her, and yet she never quit this mission of feeding the hungry.

For her, feeding the hungry started by growing vegetables in her garden and sharing them with neighbors and others whom she knew needed the food. She soon discovered the grocery store "throwaways" and added that to her growing list of items to donate. Despite this, she knew she was not reaching everyone in need.

The store manager discovered what the young woman was doing and told her that if she came to the back door at the end of the day, he would have a box with salvaged food for her. She did not have to rummage through the dumpster, like a vagabond, anymore.

Over the next 25 years, JoAnn Pike continued in her endless efforts and expansive energy to feed the hungry. She founded a distribution center where a retailer could distribute salvaged food in larger quantities. She solicited volunteers to sort and package the food to be shipped to other locations without being paid one cent. Some people walked through the door and she gave them back their dignity by giving them an opportunity to do meaning-ful work at the facility. At the end of a shift, she allowed them to take food home to feed their children.

JoAnn recruited trucking companies to help with the distribu-tion. She also met with executives of companies to convince them to raise money to buy food that could not be acquired through donations. The organization she created, Good Shepherd Food Bank (gsfb.org), continues to grow and today serves over 600 agencies in the state of Maine and feeds 70,000 people per month. All from one woman's vision and humble beginnings in her home.

In another place, a young woman in her late 20's flies to Guatemala to study Spanish and is led to a city dump where gen-erations of families are making their living. Day in and day out, mothers, fathers and children scrounge through the massive dump looking for items to salvage and sell. The money they earn buys food for their family.

This young woman had a different vision: to get the children out of the dump, give them nutritious food and educate them while their parents continued to work. After selling her car and other belongings in the U.S., this woman, Hanley Denning, began creating a safe passage for Guatemalan children to do just that. Her vision became a reality and today, Safe Passage, (safepassage.org), works to care for children who are no longer allowed in the dump.

These two modern day heroines have touched people's lives in a way many of us only dream of doing. They had a vision; a vision of hope; a vision of love; a vision of caring. JoAnn Pike passed away in 2004 at much too young an age. She was only in her 60's. Hanley Denning was killed in a tragic car accident in January of 2007 in Guatemala. She was in her late 30's. The work that these women started continues through the commitment of others who will keep their visions alive. Both visions started with a dream.

We can all make a difference in this world. We can bring hope to a child in need, a listening ear to a lonely elder or just sit with someone in their hour of pain or sorrow. We all can make a difference. Where have you made a difference? Where can you make a difference in the world today? How can you be a heroine for one person today?

The flame of the memory of JoAnn and Hanley continues to burn brightly today—may it never be extinguished. Let each one of us find ways to be heroic. It starts with a small gesture either to a stranger or someone we know in need.

Reflection Questions: Who are the heroes and heroines in your life? What makes them heroes/heroines to you? What have they taught you?

"I wait for what comes and experience the
joy and delight of the unexpected."

Staying Open to Possibility

Every day, my husband and I ask one another the same question, *"Do you think we will have a good sunset this evening?"* This is our ritual throughout the year. We live on a lake in Maine looking west to the mountains. Every night that we are home we have the opportunity to expect the unexpected and be surprised. Often, we think the sun won't break through the clouds or the sky will not appear as beautiful as other nights. But then, suddenly, we are surprised to see pinks, purples and grays light up against a backdrop of blue.

In life, we have choices. We can expect the unexpected and be pleasantly surprised, or we can assume that things will not turn out the way we hoped. I am privileged to meet and coach many people during a time of work and life transition. When I first meet a client in transition, he or she may arrive at my doorstep discouraged, angry and unsure of what the future will bring. As we begin working together, they may begin to let go and slowly start allowing themselves to see the future possibilities. This does not happen overnight. The future begins to unfold in small steps. People open the door to conversation about the future. They begin to be surprised by others' generosity of listening, sharing stories and providing support and leads for new job options.

When we are not open to possibilities, we may not experience the joy of expecting the unexpected. We may stay stuck. We may operate from a negative base of "things won't work out." We become impatient. We want things to happen under our terms and according to our timeline. When we actively wait and begin to expect the unexpected, we can experience surprise and joy.

I learned to watch the sunsets and see the beauty unfold before my eyes. I cannot rush it or predict it. I need to be patient and allow myself to let go of my expectations. Then, I wait for what comes and experience the joy and delight of the unexpected.

Reflection Questions: Do you allow yourself to expect the unexpected? How has this impacted your life?

"...the quiet, meditative and amazing act of slowing down. It was mesmerizing to watch."

Monhegan Island, September 2014.
Lincoln County, Maine.

Slowing Down the Pace

We live in a fast-paced, never enough time, "need it now" society. Information flows instantaneously. We can research any topic, buy anything or sell anything through the internet at any hour of the day or night. We can wind ourselves up and try to keep pace with the speed around us.

Or....we can take a deep breath and slow down. We can pace the amount of information we absorb and the speed at which we move through the world. We can limit the amount of "stuff" we are willing to take in over the course of a week, a day or an hour.

Recently, I facilitated development conversations with senior staff at a college. As part of the conversations, I asked people to share their own stories with me. What a wonderful gift I receive when I have an opportunity to listen and reflect back to people what I hear. Their words touching softly on my ears, their tone excited when they are talking about something that touched their soul or times in their life when they felt a deep passion for what they were doing—all are connections to my own story and others that I hear.

The interviews were scheduled back-to-back with barely enough time to eat a snack all day. During a brief break, I walked to the art center, where I witnessed meditation and art in a beautiful form. A man, hired by the college, was creating a mandala out of colored, tiny sand pebbles. He was on campus for three weeks to create this piece that would be disposed of at the end of his visit. In the meantime, it was being created by his memory in the most quiet, meditative and amazing act of slowing down. It was mesmerizing to watch.

What beauty! What inspiration! What if we all took the time in our lives and work to be meditative in doing our life's work? What richness might emerge? How contagious might it be for others? The collective energy could be amazing.

As I walked briskly through the cold, wintry air back to my interviews, I silently vowed to be more reflective in listening to the remaining stories that I was going to hear that afternoon. I vowed to take in the stories and not let my mind wander to thinking about my long drive home at the end of the day. I vowed to stay in the moment.

By consciously deciding to change how I wanted to be, a transformation occurred. I began connecting with others at a deeper level. I was open to letting information flow with a clear mind, not a cluttered mind. The richness of the conversations provided an opportunity for connection and learning about what mattered to the person across the table from me.

As I drove home, I could not get the beauty of the artwork out of my mind. The slow, deliberate and meditative work of one person creating something beautiful for all others to witness was such a gift.

Reflection Questions: What would it take for you today to slow down and weave your life journey in a deliberate fashion? Can you start small and, like sand crystals, begin to create a new world for yourself?

"I often wonder about the stories
that are shared..."

Lakehurst Community, June 2013.
Windham, Maine.

Community

In the summer, our quiet lakeside community in Maine unfurls with a wave of activity. Although most of us are year-round residents, the winter keeps us mostly indoors. Come summer, we're drawn out to our docks where we lounge by the tranquil water, wave enthusiastically to each other, and send our "hellos" across the lakefront. As we pass on our walks, we pause to greet each other and briefly catch up on family news.

In one part of our community, there is a practice that intrigues me. Several houses in a row have chairs, many just plastic well-worn chairs, in a circle on their lawns. One lawn is punctuated with white chairs, another with green and still another mix of old and new, plastic and wooden. These chairs send a message of community. The chairs invite people into the circle of conversation, storytelling and laughter. These are the sounds of connecting after a long winter; the sounds of a community of summer friends and family.

On my daily walk with my dogs, I often wonder about the stories that are shared around these circles. Are they the stories of dreams for the future, dreams lost, or stories of connections and relationships? I wonder how one is invited into the circle? How do you know when to begin or when to end?

Community brings each of us a sense of connection in a world that is full of anxiety and concern. In many ways, our world of community has grown by the use of social media, but it's the face-to-face connections that afford a real sense of understanding. A longing for community is resurfacing. Coffee shops with lounge chairs invite customers in to stay and maybe greet and talk with others, even strangers.

Neighborhoods, grange halls and churches in times past created community. People are returning to these as vehicles to build connection to others.

Over the years, I have been blessed by being a part of a variety of communities. Mostly, these communities were created by women who needed to come together to help one another through storytelling.

Recently, one of these communities reunited for an afternoon after not being together for three years. The group initially came together fifteen or twenty years ago with the assistance of a facilitator. I actually joined the community when it was transforming from a formal gathering to informal. Over the years, we have connected and reconnected at times, meeting at the home of one of the women or for brunch at some relaxing place. We share recent stories of our lives, the heartache, the joys and dreams. Then we depart, scattering to different areas of the country with hugs and smiles to hold us until the next time we come together.

In the work that I do as a facilitator, I foster opportunities to build community by having participants sit at round tables or in a circle. When people are seated classroom-style, the potential sense of community and connection is stifled.

Why does community matter? Community gives us the sense of belonging. A community provides us a way to support one another, spend time listening to what is important to others, share what is important to us and connect in a way that can keep our spirit alive. I hope you find community in your life to help during joyful and challenging times.

Reflection Questions: What does community mean to you? Where do you feel a sense of community? Who is in your circle? How do they get invited in?

"What if I did not return? What would I be
leaving behind for others to take care of?"

Davis Camp at Sabbathday Lake, 2016.
New Gloucester, Maine.

A Time for Tidying
Up Loose Ends

I am not the most organized person you will ever meet. I *am* organized in my own way, though. Significant piles of miscellaneous or important items are stacked next to my computer, night stand and art table. I know where things are most of the time. If I cannot find something, I first go to the visible piles and then retreat to the hidden stacks in the closets.

Preparing for a vacation or business trip, I am amazed at how I find myself organizing and tidying up loose ends before I leave. I am not sure if it really makes a difference with the piles, but the need is there to have everything in place.

Now, I know I am not the only one that undertakes this task. For me, it helps me transition; leaving behind lists for others (feed the birds, take the garbage out, sort the mail) and knowing that I have put most things in order, so that somehow when I return I will be starting with a fresh slate. Things that I have put off (publishing my bi-monthly newsletter) suddenly have to be completed. New contacts must be added to my subscriber list, articles for possible publications need to be sent and paintings requiring final touches need to be worked on. All of this should be finished before leaving.

Even phone calls are on the list. I need to hear my older sister's calm voice along with my two daughters' sweet voices. My sister and I always joke before one of us goes away. We have a count-down. Messages are left indicating how many days we have left to talk (although we always have our cell phones with us when we are away). It's as if we will never talk again.

This ritual of tidying up loose ends has a purpose. There is great comfort in organizing and finishing things. A sense of accomplishment is achieved. I find comfort in hearing voices for one last time before boarding a plane. What if I did not return? What would I be leaving behind for others to take care of? What loose ends would need tending to?

I would not want to burden anyone with my loose ends. My late husband left me with loose ends. He did not clean out his garage. He always said he was going to organize it. He did not clean out his drawers of old stuff. He did not take care of paperwork that needed to be reviewed and discarded. Most importantly, he did not tend to relationships that needed tending to, leaving unsettled business.

He left me with these loose ends. Oh, I have managed sorting the paperwork, cleaning out his garage when the house sold and boxing up his personal items from his drawers. I found ways to take care of the material things that needed to be organized.

What I could not tidy up were his relationships. Words unsaid, his intentions unstated to those affected, things not given away that should have been given away to loved ones from a first marriage (family heirlooms, high school mementos, photographs, old baseball mitts).

What do I do with these loose ends? Tears flow as I write these words; long, lost and sad tears of relationships torn apart. Years have passed. His things are still boxed up with the hope that one day I will know where they should go.

If not taken care of, loose ends can be painful for those left behind.

When the day comes and I do not return, I hope that I have taken care of the loose ends that matter. I hope my loved ones know my intentions. I hope I do not leave them in pain.

Reflection Questions: What loose ends do you have in your life? Which relationships need tending to?

"Look at the faces. See the joy and
see the pain and fear."

Jordan Bay, April 2015.
Windham, Maine.

Time for Compassion

The line in the department store was long, in keeping with the holiday bustle. Patient customers juggled their items in their arms or checked what they had in their carriages, making sure nothing was forgotten. Time was running out and one trip was all that would fit into many of their hectic schedules. Cashiers could barely tilt their heads upward to meet the eyes or see the faces of their harried customers.

I waited in line behind a chattering man ready to cash out in front of me. He was talking about his family members to the cashier, who he obviously knew. He was chatting about how food and paper goods were being consumed at a rapid pace. His break time was being used to purchase more milk, eggs and basic items that seemed to be diminishing quickly with extra people in his home.

Suddenly, another man accompanied by a young woman, presumably his daughter, rushed ahead in line to the register, catching the attention of the cashier just as she ended the transaction with the chatting man and began processing mine.

"Excuse me, excuse me! Did you find my wallet? I just went through here."

The cashier glanced up briefly, looked quickly around and then began reaching for my purchases to scan. In the same breath, she simply said, "Nothing left here."

"But, but you just waited on me," he stammered.

"No, it must not have been me," she replied.

"Remember, I had the fifty dollar bill," he said as he tried again to get her attention.

The cashier continued with my transaction, brushing the annoying man aside. His face showed sheer panic. Maybe the wallet contained a special photo of a loved one, or his identification cards, or maybe the only money he had left for Christmas shopping. As the cashier continued to ignore the man, he began feeling in his pockets, opening his jacket with a continued and rising look of panic and anxiety.

"Are you sure it is not here?" he tried again for her attention.

As I watched all of this unfolding, I saw the outline of what appeared to be a man's shaped wallet in an inner vest worn to keep the cold air away. There, secure in its resting place, was the missing wallet. Quietly, I asked if he had checked his inside vest. Startled, he reached in his vest pocket and felt the lost wallet.

"Thank you," he said quickly as his face softened and he turned without another word.

The cashier paused and looked into my eyes, "Thank you for helping him. We do have good people who shop here."

We all need to be reminded to slow down and watch what is going on around us. No one escapes life's struggles. We need to look at the faces. See the joy and see the pain and fear. We all need to take the time for each other. In just taking one moment, maybe we can ease someone's fear, pain or anxiety. Compassion and an outstretched hand may lend a gentler feel to troubling times and allow the good to come out in all of us.

Reflection Questions: Where have you seen someone show compassion? When have you shown compassion? What was the reaction of others? What did you learn?

"Maybe I will make a difference
in the life of someone."

Maine Lighthouse, June 2013.
Portland, Maine.

Be a Hero

I admit that I have not been inspired lately. No new stories in my head. A few weeks ago, I tried to write about the change in seasons and, later, I tried to write about traditions. But the passion was just not there. The words fell like heavy lead on paper.

With the holiday season approaching, I've put all of my decorations in their perfectly planned places. With a sense of accomplishment, I personally designed and mailed my holiday cards. Purchased presents await wrapping in paper of the season. My children are older, so the joy of surprise is long gone. Today, they delight in gift certificates to their favorite stores. The joy of hunting for the perfect gift has disappeared.

I was just not inspired this holiday season. I donated money at the front of stores when I saw the bell ringer and I sent money to those in need. Usually, I search for a family in need of assistance, but not this year. I was searching for something deeper, something different. I needed inspiration.

The local church had several signs indicating the date and time for an upcoming blood drive. I had noted the date in my calendar and wanted to make sure that I took the time to give. I give blood, but not on a regular basis. I hate needles and poking. I hate the wait. I just do not bother most of the time. As I rushed around on the day of the drive, I thought of the many reasons why I could not make time to give blood. I knew I needed to give, though. I do not know why, but I was drawn to the church.

As I walked through the door and greeted the volunteers, I was handed the forms and paperwork to read and fill out.

Oh, I really don't have the time for this.

Maybe, I can just turn around.

No, the volunteers will probably give me harsh stares.

I'm here, so I might as well stay.

With the paperwork filled out, I now had to wait. Five minutes, 10 minutes, 15 minutes went by. Finally, my name was called. I followed the nurse to a private area where I sat patiently as she checked my blood pressure and asked questions. Then, with that finished, I was told that I could return to the waiting area.

More waiting with nothing to read or distract me and my thoughts. Ten more minutes, 15 minutes, 30 minutes went by.

Okay, I have so much to do, I can't wait any longer.

What, did I hear my name?

Yes, it's my turn!

The nurse was nice and began apologizing immediately for the wait and for the additional time the blood draw would take. She would get me out as quickly as possible, as she knew I must have more important things to do.

Within a few minutes, a needle was inserted into my arm and I was connected to a bag. Drip, drip, drip. My red blood began flowing with little effort. Life blood. I was left alone, lying on the table, with just my thoughts flowing freely like my blood. Suddenly, it came to me. This is the true meaning of the season...giving. Giving freely of myself. What could be more important? What greater gift could I give this season than stopping what I was doing and taking the time to give the gift of life, my own blood?

Faith Hill, the country western singer, in one of her holiday songs, asks the question, "Where are you Christmas? Why can't I find you?" For me, as I had been going about the business of the season, making my lists, shopping, wrapping some presents and writing cards, I had lost the meaning of Christmas. As I lay on the cold table with my warm blood flowing, the meaning of Christmas began to flow through my veins. *How could I have let the meaning slip away? How had I lost it?*

Later that evening, I could not get warm. Neither the crackling logs of my fireplace nor the heat of my home's furnace seemed enough to warm me physically. But a deep emotional warmth spread through me. I felt inspired and grateful knowing that I had discovered a deeply meaningful new holiday tradition: the gift of giving my blood. How lucky I am that I have that to give!

The Red Cross calls it *being a hero*. I don't feel like a hero, but maybe I will make a difference in the life of someone this holiday season. Two hours of my time during a busy season. Two hours to reflect and be inspired. Two hours to give life to someone else. I have found Christmas.

Questions for Reflection: Have you ever lost the meaning of a holiday, tradition or something you held dear? How did you get the inspiration or meaning back? If you haven't been able to retrieve it, how might you?

"She gingerly approached me with her soft
eyes and black curly fur; 1 fell in love."

Leila, May 2004.
Windham, Maine.

Puppy Love:
Anticipation and Hope

I had never been a dog lover, or even any kind of animal lover. You see, I am allergic to animals...all animals. But in the winter of 2004, I heard a story on television about Labradoodles, a kind of dog that is allergy-friendly. Labradoodles (a mixed breed dog created by crossing the Labrador Retriever and the Standard or Miniature Poodle) were first bred in Australia for a blind woman who needed a seeing-eye dog, but she was allergic to dogs. This sparked the beginning of cross breeding the gentle lab to the intelligent and hypoallergenic poodle. The resulting mix, the Labradoodle, proved a great combination.

"This is wonderful," I thought.

My husband had passed away 17 months prior, I was in a new home and I was lonely. A non-shedding, allergy-friendly puppy seemed to be the perfect solution. I needed puppy love.

I searched on the internet and found a local breeder. I contacted her and talked about the possibilities of owning a puppy. She had a litter due soon and so I agreed to join the ranks of dog owners.

Over the next two months, my anticipation grew. I was nervous. One moment, I was happy, the next moment I was wondering if I was making a mistake. This was a big commitment for me. *Would I be a good owner? Would I have the patience? How would my life change?*

The day I picked up my new puppy, Leila, these questions filled my head. When I arrived, I held the nervously energetic new pup. She was adorable. As she gingerly approached me with her soft eyes and black curly fur, I fell in love. Puppy love.

Leila has been with me for several years now. She is pure joy. I never thought I could love an animal so much. She brings spontaneous laughter to me. She is gentle and knows when something is wrong with me. Even though it has not always been easy (she vomited all the way home on the first day, chewed furniture and left little smelly surprises for me to pick up), I do not regret my decision to bring her into my life. She gives me unconditional love.

We all need the anticipation of something new, like puppy love, in our lives. We need joy after pain. We need hope for and the joy of new experiences. Begin searching now for the possibility of bringing something new to your life and be ready for the joy.

Questions for Reflection: When was the last time you felt the joy of anticipating something new in your life? A joy that would bring hope, love and laughter?

"Yet I know that I need to toss the blanket
aside, like the wind does with the leaves."

Lakehurst Community, October 2014.
Windham, Maine.

Blanket of Leaves

I glanced sleepily out my bedroom window. The morning hour was still early and my household was quiet. For the past two days, hard rain, wind and a preview of the coming winter months beat down on us. Looking out, the trees that were once full and bursting with fall colors were now bare; their leaves now a soft blanket covering the barren, cold earth.

Despite the cold, I was drawn to leaving the warmth of my home to experience the feel and look of nature's new golden blanket. The wind might soon blow the leaves away without concern, leaving their beauty unnoticed.

I took my camera out and lay down on the ground, my body flat against the cold earth. The leaves formed their own margins, not adhering to the defined boundaries of the yard or driveway. The blanket provided a soft covering for squirrels and birds to scamper through.

A blanket is a covering and it's usually not permanent. As a noun, "blanket" is defined as *an obstruction* and as a verb, *to interfere.*

We all need blankets. They protect us and serve as warmth and comfort, and they need not be permanent. If they are, they begin to keep things out. They create a barrier between what's outside the blanket and what's under the blanket.

There are days when I do want to stay under my warm, cozy blanket in bed. It keeps the noise and the business of the day away. It gives me a sense of security and comfort. Yet, I know that I need to toss the blanket aside, like the wind does with the leaves, or I will miss out on the possibilities of the new day.

Questions for Reflection: What blankets do you keep around you? Are they for comfort and warmth or are they keeping things away? Blankets are important and have a purpose for a time. Is it time for you to throw your blanket to the wind and discover what might be out there?

"In spite of winter's remains...tender small
leaves will burst though the softening earth."

Boston Common, April 2012.
Boston, Massachusetts.

Planting Bulbs for Hope

L ooking at the purple haze on the mountains bathed in the rising sunlight, I know that the last of the warm Indian summer days are upon us. The docks and boats are retired to their winter storage. The summer visitors have long left their spoken words and smiles behind. Those endlessly warm days and cool nights are being replaced by early signs of frost. Watching the news, I learn that snow blanketed Buffalo, New York this week. I know that it will only be a short time before the first white flakes appear on my own steps.

For the first time, this fall I planted bulbs in my garden. I'm not a gardener by trade, or by any other definition. After losing my much-needed help from a dear gardener friend who is battling recurring breast cancer, I had to learn how to take care of my flower gardens by myself. Earlier this summer, I planted annuals. I weeded, watered and nurtured my flowers. I watched proudly as they burst into a rainbow of beauty over the summer months.

Why do we plant bulbs? What are we hoping for? Planting bulbs this year has given me hope for spring. The bulbs will ease me through the difficult transition from summer to autumn. The fall days are beautiful, crisp and bright. But the nights are an early reminder of the dark, cold days of winter to come.

I planted bulbs of crocuses, tulips and hyacinths, deep in the earth where they will incubate in relative warmth until the first signs of spring. Then, in spite of winter's remains and a few snowy patches, tender small leaves will burst though the softening earth.

We all need that hope. I have hope that my friend's body will heal over the winter months. I have hope that I will be witness to the signs of spring.

Questions for Reflection: Do you have an idea, hope or thought that you can incubate for the winter months that can burst into bloom in the spring? Plant your bulb of hope today and be surprised by what may come up next spring.

"...reflection can transform something familiar."

Jordan Bay in December, 2013.
Sebago Lake, Windham, Maine.

Reflections

One of my favorite things to photograph is reflections. I'm in awe of how a reflection can transform something familiar so that I may see it in a new way. I love how the sky and clouds, or a bird in flight, is reflected on the water. Even a flower's reflection appearing in a puddle after a spring rain captivates me. Reflections may be brief—clouds pass and birds fly away—but what they reveal is important and can give us such joy.

I often do not take the time to reflect on my own life. Where does the time go? When I was in my youth, I wanted to be older. Now that I am older, I ask for time to slow down. There are so many things I need and want to spend time on: photography, painting, writing, family and friends, coaching and consulting, and offering Reiki therapy.

On the days I spend with my very active and inquisitive grandson, I am fascinated by his pace. When we walk together with the pups racing ahead, he pauses, looks to the ground at a little speck or rock, and says, "*Wait just a minute; I need to look at this.*" Or, as we walk, he will stop, listen to the sounds and ask, "*What is that, Mema?*" (his name for me).

To be able to pause is a luxury today. Most of us pause for vacations, but to really pause and reflect is a greater challenge. Deciding to take time away from social media and busy lives can feel extravagant. I resigned as Chair and member of a nonprofit Board for an outstanding organization, the Good Shepherd Food Bank. Although this was a difficult decision, the time was right for me. The work will be continued by others who are very capable and who I respect.

I spent a lot of hours at the food bank. I find now I have gaps in time. The tendency is to fill the gap by joining another board or by filling the time with activities, but I am not. In my coaching practice, when clients leave a company, sell their business or have a major change, I encourage them to just pause for reflection.

Reflection can give us the time to savor the moments we've had and look forward to what might come next.

Questions for Reflection: When was the last time you paused for reflection? What did you learn about yourself?

"Maybe the real safety that we can create is a sense of knowing we have made a difference.

Hawk in Flight, October 2014.
Rattlesnake Mountain, Raymond, Maine.

Safety: Reality or Illusion?

Early one cool fall day, I prepared to make the two-hour commute to Boston for an all-day conference. The decision to drive the morning of the conference, rather than overnight in the city, meant that I would have to be up and out of bed very early if I were to arrive on time. This was a struggle for me, as I cherish my lazy, sleepy Saturday mornings. This particular Saturday there simply wasn't time for a leisurely breakfast. Still, I lingered a bit too long as I drank my coffee and gazed out at the mist-laden lake. I ended up leaving the house later than I should have.

As I traveled down the highway in my midsized sports utility vehicle (downsized due to fuel costs), I found the roads were good and the traffic was moderate. I was pleased with the progress I was making and confident that I would arrive at my destination on time. In fact, I surmised that I would even have time to stop for a coffee refill. I was enjoying my early morning outing, singing out loud to the country tunes that were playing on my favorite radio station. Suddenly, I felt a strong vibration and a loud noise emanate from my vehicle. I was in the passing lane and knew that I needed to quickly get to the breakdown lane. As my speed drastically reduced and I luckily avoided being hit by rushing cars that came from behind, I managed to maneuver my car safely to the side of the road.

As the car came to an abrupt stop, my body was shaking and I suddenly began to feel a wave of relief from the fact that no one had hit me. I emerged from the car and proceeded to inspect it. The right back rear tire had, much to my surprise, literally exploded and had begun to smolder.

What had happened? Had I failed to notice an obstacle in the road? Had I hit something that punctured my tire? I called AAA and within a short period of time the tire was replaced and I was back on the road. This time, however, I proceeded much more cautiously as I continued on to my destination.

Later, as I began to replay in my mind the events from earlier that day, I was struck by how safe and secure I had felt in my SUV. Its mere size provided me a sense of security. In many aspects of our lives, including our jobs, investments, health and relation- ships, this feeling of safety is not necessarily a reflection of reality as much as it is illusion.

In an era of global economic uncertainty and political instabil- ity, we are given reason to pause and ask, "How safe and secure are we? How safe and secure am I?"

These plunges into the depths of uncertainty have many tread- ing water and assessing their relationship with money, material goods, jobs and even relationships. What can we feel safe about? How can we thrive when turbulent waters swirl all around us?

For me, not just surviving but thriving involves a process of integrating what was, what is and what the future may hold. As with my own cancer journey, I look to understand and integrate, knowing I will never be the same. Things have changed for me. At some level, uncertainty will always be my lifelong companion as a cancer survivor.

Still, a sense of safety and security are essential to a person's wellbeing. What actions can we take to create safety, both physical and financial? Or does true safety even exist? Is it merely an illusion? For me, creating a sense of safety and security involves focusing on the simple things in life that bring me joy and assessing how my time is spent. It is looking at family, friends, community, jobs, money and material goods and asking the relevant questions, including:

- How am I spending my time?
- What can I do to nurture my relationships with family and friends?
- Am I reaching out to others or am I waiting for others to call me?
- Am I sending a card or email to family or friends whether they are in crisis or not? Am I listening to them?
- Am I finding ways to give back to the community?
- Am I sharing my good fortune with others who may be less fortunate?
- Am I working to make a difference in others' lives?
- Am I living up to my full potential?
- Am I doing work that fuels the passion in me? If not, how can I bring elements of passion into my life?
- Is my relationship with money and material goods keeping me free from anxiety?

- Am I content with what I have right in this moment, knowing my family and I have a warm home and food?
- How can I simplify my life to focus on the true enjoyment that life can bring?
- Lastly, are there things I can give away that I no longer need?

Life is how we spend our time now, not in the future, as we never know what the future may hold. Safety is an illusion we create; letting go of that illusion can release us from striving to hold onto the things in life that may not bring us true joy. Focusing on family, friends and giving back can bring us the wealth that money and material goods cannot. Maybe, the real safety that we can create is a sense of knowing we have made a difference.

Questions for Reflection: Where do you hold the illusion of safety? What would happen if you let go of it?

"Do you have a minute?
I have a story to tell you."

Our Home, 2015.
Windham, Maine.

Where Do Memories Belong?

The day was beautiful. My husband and I were headed to the mountains to take photos of the fall foliage when we stopped at a local convenience store to grab a couple snacks. While I waited in the car, my cell phone rang. Not wanting to disrupt our day, yet not wanting to miss a call that might be important, I reached for the phone. My oldest daughter's number appeared on the screen, and I was glad I decided to take the call.

"Hi Mom. What are you doing?"

"Headed to take pictures of fall leaves," I responded.

"I have a question for you. Do you want my porcelain dolls? Since I moved into our new house, I have not opened the box they are packed in. I wanted to see if you wanted them before I gave them away."

My heart stopped. I felt my face flush. Her dolls? What was she saying? She did not want her dolls? The dolls I had given her every Christmas since she was a young child? What did she mean? How could she not want them?

My words stumbled off my lips, "Of course, I want them. They are worth a lot of money." As if she would know what that meant, but these were the only words I could find.

"Great. I will drop them off this week. Have a good day out and about," she said in her cheery voice, having no idea the impact her words had on me.

"I will. Good-bye," I quickly said as I fought back tears.

My husband returned to the car. As he climbed in, he sensed something was very wrong and asked, "What happened?"

Through tears, I recounted the details of the phone call, anger rising up in my voice.

His soothing words came quickly, "She does not know the meaning. I am so sorry you are hurt."

A week later, my daughter brought the box of dolls, precious to me, to our house. She left them in our entryway and I later carried them to the spare bedroom. I did not look at them. I just sat the box down.

Late one afternoon, before my husband came home from work, I walked with slight trepidation into the room. I sat on the floor next to the box. Could I open it? Did I dare? Yes, I needed to open it.

I opened the lid and peeked in. Yes, there they were. A rush of tears and memories hit me like an emotional storm. Here was the one that looked like her when she was five. Here was the one that reminded me of her being mischievous. Here was the one with the ponytails. Here was the Winnie the Pooh doll that was one of my favorites. As I took each doll out, I caressed its face, untangled the hair or ribbon on its head and smoothed out its clothing.

Tears flowed and then stopped. I began to just enjoy each doll. I began to think about the time that I had purchased each one. I was a single mom when my girls were little. Each year before Christmas my best friend, Donna, and I would go Christmas shopping together. As part of our annual trip, our first stop would be at a quaint doll shop in a little town in Maine. We would love to take our time looking for a doll that reminded us of my daughter. Some years, I had only enough money to purchase a small accessory for one of the dolls already in her collection.

As I sat and looked at the sweet and funny faces of these precious dolls, I began to laugh as I remembered the wonderful times I shared with my best friend. With the laughter came the realization that the memories were mine. My daughter did not know the meaning the dolls held for me. To her, they were nicely made collectibles she once appreciated but had outgrown. I realized that for me, the dolls were tangible reminders of trips with my best friend, who years later moved away, and markers from my daughter's growing up years. I let go of the anger towards my daughter for not wanting the dolls and not understanding my attachment.

I picked up the phone, "Donna, do you have a minute? I have a story to tell you."

We laughed and cried as we shared *our* memory of the dolls. Yes, they are home with me now, complete with a story about each one.

Questions for Reflection: What memories of others are you holding? What are your own? What do you need to let go of?

"Be patient with yourself; trust in the Universe; find mentors; know that you can achieve whatever you set out to do."

October Sunrise, 2015.
Standish, Maine.

Turn the Page

for Bob and Jeff

B eep, beep, beep. Oh, I just wanted to ignore the alarm. My husband, Jeff, gently nudged me and said, "Come on, it's time."

I rolled over trying to ignore him and the knowledge that it was only 4:30 am. *We are on vacation*, I thought. Then I remembered. I had wanted a shot of a sunrise for my book and with the high humidity in Maine, I knew that the sunrise would be beautiful on the lake. We only see sunsets so getting a shot of the sunrise meant rising early and driving to the other side of the lake. I had asked Jeff if he would go with me. Knowing he is such a willing partner on my adventures, I knew he would say yes and make sure we were up in time. We loaded our dogs, grabbed some coffee and we were off.

To my delight, we found the perfect location exactly due east for a morning shot. I was awed by the quiet beauty of a sunrise. When we arrived back home, I knew I was ready to write my last chapter.

Life has not been easy in our family. We have had more tragedies than many and people give pause when they hear we have had
but one more. We are resilient, though. We go on.

In 2007, I was diagnosed with breast cancer. Two years later I
had my ovaries removed and in the same year my thyroid went out
of whack. Then, on a hot July day in 2010, I was walking barefoot
up the steps from our dock. My feet were burning. Assuming they
were simply sunburned, I gave this little thought. But then, after
three months of being prodded by doctors and numerous tests for
lung and brain cancer, what I thought was sunburn was diagnosed
as neuropathy. For the next three years, I fought pain up my legs and
arms with no clear explanation of the cause. The pain was intense
when my feet hit the floor in the morning. The nerve pain radiated
up my legs and arms. As a former athlete, I struggled with accepting
that I would be like this for the rest of my life. Then, in 2013, I met
the most wonderful physical therapist who helped me to get my
physical life back. He worked with me on setting goals and listened
when I was discouraged by not making enough progress as quickly
as I would have liked. He helped me to understand that, though I
may not be able to run, I could still swim and bike and take steps to
reclaim my physical, active life. I am forever grateful to him.

As I reflect on my life and the long path that has led to publication of this book, I know several things to be true for I have seen
these truths manifested in my own and others' journeys.

First and foremost, be patient with yourself as you face life's
challenges and do your best to hold onto hope for the future.
Things happen for a reason, even though we may not know what
it is at the time.

Trust in the Universe. When you put your intentions into the Universe, they show up. Not always in the timeframe that you want because, I believe, we do not always understand the timing of the Universe. It will happen.

Know when to "turn the page." My late husband, Bob, used this phrase many times. To him, and to me, it means to know when to let go and move on. Don't get stuck on the things that do not matter.

Engage in life, which is what my husband, Jeff, reminds me to do when I am feeling I am not making progress. We found each other in 2004 and joined our lives in marriage in 2008. When I say that I am not getting anything done, he will remind me I have, indeed, been "engaging in life." I am so thankful I have Jeff in my life to share my adventures.

Lastly, know that you can achieve whatever you set out to do. This may be a physical, emotional, spiritual or professional goal. Whatever it is, you have the potential in you to achieve your goal. Just begin.

Reflection Questions: Do you know when to "turn the page"? How are you "engaging in life"?

REFLECTION
QUESTIONS

The following list restates questions that appear individually at the end of each chapter within this book. The questions are designed to challenge assumptions, create internal dialogue, and inspire you to think about your life in compelling new ways. May the blank journaling pages included in the second half of this book, along with these reflection questions which can be used as writing prompts to get you started, be useful tools in the exploration of your thoughts and feelings or as part of a book group discussion. Writing the true stories in this book has inspired, taught and healed me. I hope you will be similarly affected by exploring and recording your own stories in these pages.

Ch.1 Living a Passionate Life: Take Flight

Reflection Question: When has fear prevented you from trying something new? What would you do if fear did not hold you back?

Ch. 2 Vulnerability, Authenticity and Passion

Reflection Question: When have you felt vulnerable? When did you need help? Did your vulnerability show what you are passionate about? If so, how can you bring that passion into your life?

Ch. 3 Joy/Pain...Living in Both

Reflection Question: Where are you experiencing pain in your life? Where do you see joy as a sign of hope for future days to come? Is it in the rising sun, in a flower holding on before the cold winter days, in the beauty of a sunset or in the sound of laughter from a child?

Ch. 4 Build it Anyway

Reflection Question: What is your dream? What do you want to build? What might be stopping you from realizing your dream? Storms will come and they will pass. Begin to build today.

Ch. 5 Relay for Life: One Night's Journey

Reflection Question: Life presents challenges to us. When have you had to push through? When have you had to endure emotional or physical pain and overcome it?

Ch. 6 Intentions vs. Resolutions

Reflection Question: How do you start each year? Do you lament over old problems or look to the future? What are your intentions?

Ch. 7 An Unexpected Journey Begins

Reflection Question: When have you had unexpected news? In what way did you put trust in the Universe?

Ch. 8 Taking Risk...Taking Flight

Reflection Questions: What risk are you willing to take in your life to fuel your own sustenance for your soul? What step can you take, even if it is a small step? Who can support you?

Ch. 9 All About Time

Reflection Questions: When have you felt time moved too quickly or slowly? When have you felt too busy? What is your relationship with time?

Ch. 10 Being Still and Letting Go

Reflection Question: At certain times in our lives, we need to be still. When have you needed to be still? Did you find practicing stillness difficult? What did you learn about yourself?

Ch. 11 Growing Takes Courage

Reflection Questions: When have you had to show courage? What did you lean into? Who helped you?

Ch. 12 How Two Modern Day Heroines Made a Difference

Reflection Questions: Who are the heroes and heroines in your life? What makes them heroes/heroines to you? What have they taught you?

Ch. 13 Staying Open to Possibility

Reflection Questions: Do you allow yourself to expect the unexpected? How has this impacted your life?

Ch. 14 Slowing Down the Pace

Reflection Questions: What would it take for you today to slow down and weave your life journey in this fashion? Can you start small and, like sand crystals, begin to create a new world for yourself?

Ch. 15 Community

Reflection Questions: What does community mean to you? Where do you feel a sense of community? Who is in your circle? How do they get invited in?

Ch. 16 A Time for Tidying Up Loose Ends

Reflection Questions: What loose ends do you have in your life? Which relationships need tending to?

Ch. 17 Time for Compassion

Reflection Questions: Where have you seen someone show compassion? When have you shown compassion? What was the reaction of others? What did you learn?

Ch. 18 Be a Hero

Questions for Reflection: Have you ever lost the meaning of a holiday, tradition or something you held dear? How did you get the inspiration or meaning back? If you haven't been able to retrieve it, how might you?

Ch. 19 Puppy Love: Anticipation and Hope

Questions for Reflection: When was the last time you felt the joy of anticipating something new in your life? A joy that would bring hope, love and laughter?

Ch. 20 Blanket of Leaves

Questions for Reflection: What blankets do you keep around you? Are they for comfort and warmth or are they keeping things away? Blankets are important and have a purpose for a time. Is it time for you to throw your blanket to the wind and discover what might be out there?

Ch. 21 Planting Bulbs for Hope

Questions for Reflection: Do you have an idea, hope or thought that you can incubate for the winter months that can burst into bloom in the spring? Plant your bulb of hope today and be surprised by what may come up next spring.

Ch. 22 Reflections

Questions for Reflection: When was the last time you paused for reflection? What did you learn about yourself?

Ch. 23 Safety: Reality or Illusion?

Questions for Reflection: Where do you hold the illusion of safety? What would happen if you let go of it?

Ch. 24 Where Do Memories Belong?

Questions for Reflection: What memories of others are you holding? What are your own? What do you need to let go of?

Ch. 25 Turn the Page

Reflection Questions: Do you know when to "turn the page"? How are you "engaging in life"?

JOURNAL

JOURNAL

JOURNAL

JOURNAL

JOURNAL

JOURNAL

JOURNAL

JOURNAL

JOURNAL

JOURNAL

JOURNAL

JOURNAL

JOURNAL

JOURNAL

RESOURCES

Following is a list of Maine-based and national nonprofits that hold special meaning in my life. These organizations are committed to helping others with physical, emotional or spiritual needs. My own experiences as a volunteer with these nonprofits have been deeply meaningful, and they are mentioned in the stories I share in this book.

American Cancer Society
www.cancer.org
Nationwide organization dedicated to eliminating cancer by funding life-saving research and providing cancer education and services to patients and their families in their local communities.

Cancer Community Center
www.cancercommunitycenter.org
The mission of the South Portland, Maine based Cancer Community Center is to support and promote the well-being of people living with cancer, their families and their friends.

Dempsey Center for Cancer Hope & Healing
www.dempseycenter.org
Located in Lewiston, Maine, The Dempsey Center for Cancer Hope & Healing provides free support, education and wellness services to anyone impacted by cancer.

International Association of Reiki Professionals (IARP®)
www.iarp.org
The International Association of Reiki Professionals® is the professional association of the global Reiki community.

Feeding America
www.feedingamerica.org
The Feeding America network is the nation's largest domestic hunger-relief organization. Through a nationwide network of member food banks, Feeding America provides meals to virtually every community in the United States and works to engage our country in the fight to end hunger.

Good Shepherd Food Bank
www.gsfb.org
The Good Shepherd Food Bank works to eliminate hunger in Maine by sourcing and distributing nutritious food to people in need, building strong community partnerships, and mobilizing the public in the fight to end hunger. Working with partner agencies including food pantries, meal sites, shelters, senior centers, schools and other community programs throughout the state, Good Shepherd Food Bank helps to feed people from every county in Maine.

Safe Passage
www.safepassage.org
Safe Passage empowers the poorest, at-risk children of families working in the community of the Guatemala City Garbage Dump, by creating opportunities and fostering dignity through the power of education. Safe Passage is a 501(c)(3) nonprofit organization headquartered in Yarmouth, Maine.

Made in the USA
Columbia, SC
01 May 2017